BAPTISM *and the* COVENANT OF GRACE

BAPTISM *and the* COVENANT OF GRACE

A Pastor's Case for Baptism of Believers' Children

MICHAEL ALLEN ROGERS

One King Press
307 N. Oak Street
Lititz, PA 17543

www.onekingpress.com

Baptism and the Covenant of Grace | Michael Allen Rogers

Library of Congress Control Number: 2022943960

ISBN 979-8-9865464-0-7 Print
ISBN 979-8-9865464-1-4 eBook

Cover image and frontispiece credits: Shutterstock
Cover and frontispiece design by Hannah Linder Designs
Photograph of the author courtesy of Westminster Presbyterian Church Archives, Eve Sypien photographer

1 3 5 7 9 10 8 6 4 2

Contents

Preface   VII

1. The Significance of Baptism   1

2. Thinking about Baptism on a Clean Slate   7

3. The Covenant of Grace   19

4. Signs of the Covenant, Old and New   29

5. Additional Evidences   37

6. What is Unique about a Believer's Covenant   51
   Child?

7. Can We Have Peace About Baptism?   61

8. Baptism as Taught in Reformed Creeds   69

9. Commonly Asked Baptism Questions   75

About the Author   85

Preface

November 17, 1963: The Sunday prior to President Kennedy's assassination.

Barefoot and wearing a white robe, I stood with a small group of teenagers and adults at the front of my childhood Baptist church. We were not portraying angels in a Christmas pageant. We were candidates waiting to publicly profess our faith in Christ by means of immersion baptism.

One by one we cautiously descended the porcelain steps into the baptistry tank where our pastor waited, his beckoning smile calming our nerves. With his white shirt and necktie tucked into fisherman's waders, he drew each of us in turn to stand near him in the waist-high water.

My moment finally arrived. "Michael Rogers, do you believe in the Lord Jesus Christ as your only Savior from sin?"

"Yes...I do."

"Then in obedience to the command of our Lord in his Word, I baptize you in the name of the Father, the Son, and the Holy Ghost."

I grasped the pastor's forearm with both hands. With a practiced move, he placed a handkerchief over my nose and mouth, lowered me under the water, and raised me upright again. Spluttering and groping for a deacon's guiding hand, I sloshed up the steps, silently rejoicing in the grace of God.

Ecclesiastes 12:12 states, "Of making many books there is no end." This is surely true for books written about Christian baptism. Since apostolic days both brief tracts and full scholarly tomes on the subject have consumed entire forests for paper. Why would anyone add to this publishing blizzard?

My reason for writing comes from my long experience as a pastor. Years ago I realized that, when it comes to controversial subjects, people are more likely to be persuaded to read a booklet penned by a pastor they know and trust than one written by a stranger.

So my initial goal was to place into the hands of my congregation a relatively short, easy-reading volume of biblical reasoning as to why believers in Christ should consider their covenant children as proper subjects for baptism. For, while many of us believe this is an entirely scriptural practice, others join our congregation from differing viewpoints. And the New Testament case supporting our practice is definitely not a matter of pointing to a few simplistic Bible proof texts. In fact, I have often thought how wonderful it would be if the Book of Acts contained a single verse that read, *"And whenever the apostles baptized new converts, they included the family's infant children in accordance with the covenant of grace."* That would completely nullify the controversy. But lacking any such black-and-white biblical statement, the matter requires thoughtful, step-by-step reasoning from God's Word.

I assure you in advance that I will uncover nothing entirely novel to say on the subject. The arguments and evidence I will muster can be found in many other published resources. John Murray's *Christian Baptism* (Presbyterian and Reformed Publishing, 1970) presents classic Reformed reasoning on paedobaptism. But not everyone will find Murray to be easy reading. I have sought to conjure up a volume that might cast his doctrinal substance into a more popular reading style.

Seeking a Biblical Position on Baptism

Almost sixty years following my own teenage baptism, I am now a Presbyterian Church in America (PCA) minister who has baptized scores of adults and perhaps two hundred young children of believers. In forty years of ministry, I have never owned a pair of fisherman's waders – because I have never immersed anyone. And I've long realized that this is a subject upon which other evangelicals who love God's inerrant Word as I do differ with my theology and pastoral practice.

It stirs their curiosity when people to whom I preach learn that I believe the Bible is God's infallible Word, and that I was raised in a Baptist church and was myself baptized by immersion as a teenager, yet I baptize children of believing parents. What made me change my thinking on this subject?

Certainly I never will disparage my own believer's baptism by immersion. Why would I do that? It was a meaningful step in my growth as a disciple of Jesus Christ. Today I stand with many Christians persuaded by Scripture that a born-again consenting adult's total immersion is *one* acceptable approach to baptism – but not the *only* pathway. If an adult who has never been baptized approaches the local church pastor and elders, then he or she should be baptized as a believer before church membership is conferred.

However, we believe the Word of God also supports baptism for infant children of believing parents, performed well before a child can personally profess Christ-centered faith. And we believe the amount of water applied simply is not an arguable issue based upon clear evidence in the New Testament. Sprinkling or pouring of water in the name of the Trinity fulfills the biblical pattern just as well as immersion.

In February 2000 I preached three sermons on infant baptism to my congregation at Westminster Presbyterian Church of Lancaster, Pennsylvania. Those messages were titled "The Meaning of Baptism," "Who Should be Baptized?" and "Can We Have Peace About Baptism?" The messages definitely struck a nerve, as cassette tape copies flew off the rack for weeks afterward. When those sermons became the foundation for the first edition of this book, our first printing was exhausted within a year. Since then, *Baptism and the Covenant of Grace* has been given to hundreds of folks in our ten-week membership classes. Now I have once more revised the work, attempting greater clarity here in this third edition.

In our PCA congregation, I estimate that perhaps 15 percent of our members politely and peacefully disagree with us on the subject of infant baptism. Happily, we seem to be able to discuss the subject with grace and mutual tolerance. Membership in our church does not require total agreement on this secondary doctrine which we do not deem to be essential to salvation. (However, our ordained elders and deacons must consent to baptism of believers' children, since as spiritual leaders they are required to endorse the entire Westminster Confession of Faith.)

For those who do disagree, the primary point of conflict is usually not about total immersion as the exclusive mode of administering baptism. Dissenters generally argue that, regardless of the amount of water used, a baptismal candidate must first be *a believer* who can consciously, rationally profess faith in Jesus Christ as Lord. That is commonly referred to as a *baptistic* position: the view that personal faith in Christ must precede baptism, making infants ineligible. The position that I and many others hold is called *paedobaptist*, meaning child baptism is recognized for children of believers.

I hope you will find in these pages a reasoned case presented without rancor. I have no ax to swing at my baptistic brothers and sisters. I ask that together we might consider the meaning of biblical baptism in a prayerful, humble attitude, asking for God's light to shine on a difficult subject. May we banish a negative, argumentative spirit. Let our eyes be upon Christ, who first gave the command to baptize in the name of the Father, Son, and Holy Spirit.

For those who may want to read further on this topic, I recommend Robert Booth, *Children of the Promise* (P&R, 1995). Booth does a very fine job tracing the doctrine of the covenant of grace through all of Scripture in greater detail than I undertake here. For a treatment even more concise than mine, you might read John P. Sartelle's booklet, *What Christian Parents Should Know About Infant Baptism* (P&R, 1985).

Special acknowledgments are due to others for assistance in this work. My editor, Nancy Sayre, deserves high commendation for her skilled guidance in polishing my grammar for public viewing. My wife, Carol, also provides constant encouragement and technical support in my writing tasks. In pursuit of budding love for her, this naïve Baptist youth first entered an evangelical Presbyterian worship service at her home church in 1966. Poking my head down that rabbit hole and looking around was not unlike the experience of Alice tumbling into Wonderland. I discovered a dazzling world of historic Reformed theology and worship, and I would never be the same again.

Chapter One

The Significance of Baptism

A COLD WINTER DAY in January 1527 was also a dark day for true Christianity. Two oarsmen rowed a boat to the center of the Limmat River in Switzerland. They paused their rowing to lift a third man, bound with chains fastened to iron weights, from his prone position in the bottom of the skiff. The rowers hoisted the powerless man over the gunwale with a splash. He quickly sank and drowned.

The victim in our story was Felix Manz. His only crime was being a leader in the Mennonite faction of the Anabaptist movement, the right wing of the Protestant Reformation. Tragically, those who killed Manz were fellow sons of the Reformation who took severe objection to the Mennonite idea that claimed only a believer's baptism by immersion was legitimate. Historical witnesses report that as Felix Manz sank beneath the river that day, some riverbank onlookers cruelly cheered, "Let him who believes one must 'go under' the water, go under to stay!"

Anabaptism entered the vocabulary of Christianity as a derisive term used by its opponents in the Reformation era. It simply meant "to baptize again." Anabaptists believed Luther and Calvin did not go far enough in their separation from the errors of Rome. They viewed all infant baptisms as hopeless ceremonial relics of Roman Catholic superstition from which the true church of Christ should be purged. So they conferred a second adult baptism upon one another, usually by full immersion, to signify personal commitment to Christ as adult disciples. Where I live today in Lancaster, Pennsylvania, the descendants of Christians like Felix Manz are literally my neighbors. Daily encounters with their horse-drawn buggies on rural roads remind me of the courage of these people to stand apart from the secular world in what they regard as biblical convictions, regardless of what it costs them.

When we witness a Christian baptism, we witness one of two things. Either a person of some maturity is openly professing faith in Jesus as Lord, or we are welcoming the child of believing parents into the family of the visible church – in the hope that the child himself will one day personally affirm the gospel faith his parents have affirmed, based on the nurture of church and family.

Any Christian baptism should be an exciting worship moment, an occasion full of hope for how God may be glorified in that life. Yet the joy tends to be muted when we consider how Christians have struggled for centuries to even carry on a civil discourse about baptism. Shamefully, controversy on this issue has often divided God's people. It's been said that if you put five Christians of various denominations in a room to discuss baptism, you will discover at least six opinions on the subject. So we will explore these questions together:

- Why do we baptize at all?

- Who should be baptized?

- Does the Bible teach a clear doctrine as to what this sacrament means?

Baptism as Emphasized by Jesus

Abandoning baptism altogether as a hopelessly controversial subject is not an option for one very good reason: Jesus Christ himself laid great importance upon the practice of baptism, both at the beginning and conclusion of his earthly ministry. If we respect any teaching Jesus emphasized as being a keynote of Christianity, we must hold baptism in high regard, just as he did.

In Matthew 3:13-17, we discover Jesus implicitly endorsing a form of baptism by submitting to it himself as his cousin John was baptizing people in the Jordan River, signifying their general repentance before God. We read, "Then Jesus came from Galilee to the Jordan to John, to be baptized by him." But John tries to deter him, saying, "I need to be baptized by you, and do you come to me?" Jesus replies, "Let it be so for now, for thus it is fitting for us to fulfill all righteousness." Then John consents. As soon as Jesus is baptized, he comes up out of the water. At that moment heaven opens, and he sees the Spirit of God somehow visibly descending like a dove upon him. And a voice from heaven says, "This is my Son, whom I love; with whom I am well pleased."

Baptism as practiced by John in the desert was not quite the same as Christian baptism, since the entire gospel drama of atonement for sin at the Cross was yet to be enacted. John's baptism was simply a radical call to repentance. People were asked to turn towards the Lord Jehovah, showing real remorse for sins committed against him. This was a preparation for full gospel faith in Christ crucified, as our atonement for sin.

Of course, Jesus did not personally need to repent. He seems to acknowledge this in his brief exchange of words with John. Yet he still sought baptism as a dramatic way of identifying with sinners. We sense he was beginning to submit to the Father's will in this by stepping into our place as a sinner's substitute, which he later did fully at the Cross. The name of the Trinity was not spoken by John at Jesus' baptism. However, in that scene at the Jordan River, all three persons of the Trinity were uniquely and dramatically present: the Son submitting, the Spirit descending in powerful enablement, and the Father audibly speaking approval.

After that day and throughout Jesus' remaining public ministry, he placed very little direct emphasis on baptism. Jesus himself apparently did not baptize those who responded in faith to his ministry. But the subject resurfaces as somewhat of a surprise after the Lord's resurrection. In Matthew 28:18 and 19, shortly before Jesus ascended to heaven, we hear the Great Commission, his last instruction to disciples: "All authority in heaven and on earth has been given to me. Go therefore and make disciples of all nations, baptizing them in the name of the Father and of the Son and of the Holy Spirit, teaching them to observe all that I have commanded you." Baptism was now the Lord's imperative kingdom command, not a mere suggestion.

Based on these two occurrences from his lifetime, we can summarize that baptism was important to Jesus for three reasons. First, he submitted to it as our human example. Second, as the result of his own baptism he was empowered by receipt of "the Holy Spirit without limit," and John promised that Jesus would baptize others in this same Holy Spirit. Third, he firmly commanded baptism in the Triune name as a sign of discipleship. Surely, any ordinance holding such prominence in the life of Jesus is something we dare not trivialize or neglect.

At the very least, then, we can agree that baptism is an act of obedience to Christ. We might submit to it simply because our Lord commands us to, and call that reason enough. Anything our Savior commands needs no further rationale for support. In addition, we reciprocate Jesus' willingness to stand with us as sinners by taking our stand with him.

In baptism we eagerly tell the world we stand with Christ as our Sin Bearer and Savior. We are set aside from mere worldly persons as his own covenant possessions.

Chapter Two

Thinking about Baptism on a Clean Slate

IN DEVELOPING A GOOD definition of anything, an important first step is to clear up any mistaken notions, myths, or wrong definitions clinging to the subject. So we pause here to denounce some wrong ideas that are taught or implied about baptism – ideas which cannot be supported by the Bible. Because we all are products of our families and past environment, many of us have misinformation rattling around in our minds regarding baptism that should be either unlearned or set aside before we can arrive at a Bible-based understanding. To that end, consider each of the following statements:

1. Receiving baptism is not essential to salvation. If I were to face God on the final Day of Judgment unbaptized, I would be in no greater disadvantage than was the thief on the cross who Jesus said would immediately upon his death inherit paradise. Without baptism, that guilty sinner entered heaven that very day according to a sure promise of Jesus. Likewise, all Old Testament saints who trusted Jehovah in true faith were saved apart from any act of water baptism. Baptismal waters never touched the brows of Abraham, Sarah, Moses, or David, yet they were redeemed by looking for the promised Messiah who was yet to come. So while baptism is important, God can and does save apart from it, as he sovereignly determines to do whenever faith in the atoning work of Christ is present or incipient in a person's life.

2. Baptism never directly conveys divine salvation by its mere physical application. Here we differ sharply with the Church of Rome and some other denominations. Baptism is a spiritual sign and seal, but the symbol should never be confused with the reality to which it points. This means we do not endorse "baptismal regeneration," the notion that the physical act of baptism saves the soul of the recipient.

To illustrate, if I am on the Pennsylvania Turnpike heading east towards metro Philadelphia, and I see just ahead of me a large green sign announcing "Philadelphia – 12 miles," I would not point at the sign and tell my passenger, "Look there, that six-by-twelve-foot green steel rectangle must be Philadelphia." Of course not. We both understand the difference between a green and white road sign that only announces the city's proximity, and the actual metropolis of steel, asphalt, brick, and mortar. Why then can we not make a similar separation between baptism as an outward symbol pointing the way to salvation in Christ and the inward, spiritual reality it visually represents?

Many people who advocate a believers-only view of baptism assume that all Protestants who are willing to baptize infants expect that saving grace is mysteriously bestowed upon the child in the physical act of baptism. Count me out! The Roman Church teaches this, and I have met Anglicans and Lutherans who seem to be pretty much on the same page. But that most definitely is not the position of paedobaptists. Baptismal regeneration (the idea that the act of baptism confers the new birth of faith) is a notion we denounce loud and clear. I do so at every baptism service. Since we believe it cannot be defended from the Bible's teaching, we ought not be indicted with the errors of others. In one's zeal to throw out the dirty bathwater of historic religious superstitions and abuses of baptism, we need not throw away the baby, too. Infant baptism of the believer's child can be practiced without making the mistake of saying that it immediately bestows the grace which it, in fact, only symbolizes.

3. Baptism's value is not measured by whether or not the ritual is "meaningful" to me. Baptism is never a badge of spiritual achievement. This error tends to be committed by those who argue for believers-only baptism. They often say, "But being baptized as an infant did not mean anything to me. I had no faith, and I don't even think my parents were born again at the time. So now I want to be baptized when I know I have conscious trust in Christ and I can claim something I fully understand." The obvious problem in that objection is how this thinking revolves entirely around me. Look at me. I have trusted in Jesus. I am ready to wear the merit badge of baptism. Probably no one would ever characterize it quite so crudely as that, but they often imply as much.

The plain symbolism of water baptism outwardly represents God washing us by his internal regeneration as the blood of Jesus Christ pays the debt of our redemption and cleanses us from sin. It is God who designs his work in eternal election by grace alone, and it is God whose Holy Spirit awakens us from our helpless deadness in sins to give us a new birth. Ephesians 2:8 says, "For by grace you have been saved through faith. And this is not your own doing; it is the gift of God, not a result of works, so that no one may boast." It cannot be emphasized enough: God saves when and where and how he determines, even apart from my own consciousness certified in the act of baptism.

Evangelicals are sometimes guilty of placing too much emphasis upon fixing a certain moment of one's conscious "decision" for Christ, which may or may not be possible to precisely mark with a calendar date. In new member interviews with adults, I ask for a simple account of their relationship to Christ as Lord. Many begin by somewhat defensively saying, "Well, Pastor, I have to admit I cannot give you a calendar date for my conversion..." They are nervous that they may fail my test by such a reply. To that, I answer: "Fine. Let's just begin with who Jesus Christ is to you right now, today." Then we can gently peel back layers of their spiritual autobiography to learn how they arrived at a position of present-day trust in the Lord.

Today, as I write in my seventies, I believe I can identify a week of summer vacation Bible school in June 1957 as my first memorable encounter with God's grace in Christ at the Cross of Calvary – when I sensed that Jesus died for me. I was 8 years old when a spiritual stirring by the Holy Spirit awakened and convicted me through a Bible lesson taught by Mrs. Schwartz, the red-haired, blue-eyed mother of a friend. Later that afternoon, I knelt alone under a tree in my back yard and prayed fervently, saying "Yes' to Jesus as my Lord and Savior.

Although I still estimate that summer encounter in 1957 as the clearest memorable landmark for my 8-year-old "decision" for Christ, had you asked me on the day of my believer's baptism six years later to fix the date I was "saved," my 14-year-old soul might not have been so sure of the absolute moment. For I did endure the typical adolescent struggle with assurance of my salvation on and off between the ages of 8 and 14. At the time of my baptism, I might have been accurately classified as yet a spiritual "infant." God had dealt with me in more of a gradual awakening process from my childhood through teenage years, unlike the lightning strike of transformational grace visited upon Saul of Tarsus on the road to Damascus.

Our feelings can take time to catch up with realities of the mind and heart. So, is it right to insist that, above all other criteria, my baptism should be based mainly upon a calendar experience of 100% Grade-A certifiably felt trust in Christ? I know of Baptist churches that will welcome children as young as 5 or 6 years old to receive what they call a "believer's" baptism. But at what point does any human being who is still below the onset of puberty, who is unable yet to comprehend the multiplication tables, become a certified believer expected to testify with sufficient intellectual gravitas about a saving work that God the Holy Spirit has completed in his soul?

In fact, long before we are prepared to respond, God's Spirit initiates saving grace in our spiritually dead souls. God takes sovereign initiative to incubate spiritual life in us. In the same way, and according to the mystery of God's sovereign will, many of us believe that eternal salvation may apply to pre-born infants who are miscarried or aborted. And the Lord may work by his grace in mentally deficient human beings who will never have a fully rational capacity to express a "decision" to trust in Christ.

Therefore, the act of baptism should not be based entirely upon my presenting to the church an articulate "testimony" of my spiritual conversion experience. The glory of the matter belongs not to what we can humanly testify to, but to what the Triune God wonderfully and mysteriously does via the Spirit's inward surgery, applying to souls the gospel of Jesus Christ.

4. Baptism, whether administered to an infant or an adult, cannot guarantee that the recipient will be finally saved. In our human fallible judgment, pastors and elders decide who shall be baptized in a local church. And I can guarantee that we as spiritual leaders have in the past and will again administer baptism to some who may eventually prove to be eternally lost. Does this shock you? Baptists may criticize infant baptism by asking, "How can you possibly know that child will grow up to be a Christian?" Our answer: "Of course we cannot know such a thing with certainty. But at least in the case of believers' children, we do act upon the best possible presumption."

How do we know with certainty that a 25-year-old woman who appears to be full of fervent love for the Lord when she requests a believer's baptism is indeed truly saved? Her words of profession seem entirely sincere, so we accept her profession at face value because we cannot see the heart. But consider Acts 8:9-24, which tells about Simon the Magician who came to the apostles full of gospel enthusiasm. Or so it seemed. The text says, "Even

Simon himself believed, and after being baptized he continued with Philip" (13). In some manner he displayed what superficially appeared to the judgment of apostles to be saving faith. But then it quickly turned out that his zeal for Christ had a very false foundation, since Simon asked how he could join the apostles in producing supernatural healings from his own bag of magic tricks. Peter turned on Simon and told him, "You have neither part nor lot in this matter, for your heart is not right before God" (21).

And we never do find out whether this man afterward made true repentance by presenting a much-humbled and genuine profession of faith. Simon's unfinished story tells of a baptized man who to all appearances may have permanently remained a spiritual castaway, not a saved disciple of Jesus.

Therefore, if you think it is somehow safer to baptize only those who make a mature-sounding profession of faith, consider this: all baptisms are administered upon the presumption, or human hope, that saving faith is either present now, or may be forthcoming in the future. It is always possible that we will presume incorrectly and discover that we have baptized a mere professing believer who eventually proves to be a hypocrite. Or we could baptize a covenant child who does not endorse his parents' devotion to Christ for decades, but then sincerely turns to the Lord late in his own adult years. This question, then, becomes of preeminent importance:

is our presumption about each and every baptismal candidate well founded or not?

In forty years as a pastor, I have presided over several disciplinary excommunications. These people had variously joined the congregation via infant baptism combined with a teenage communicants class testimony, or by adult baptism based upon what seemed at the time to be a convincing testimony of faith. Regardless of how they came into our membership, their later unrepentant sin or overt denials of the faith pressed church elders to come to an awesome (and awful) verdict: that these individuals' present actions gave convincing evidence that they were outside the fold of humble redemption in Christ. So their memberships in the congregation was annulled – but only after careful investigation and leaders' multiple appeals for repentance fell upon deaf ears.

Dr. Benjamin B. Warfield, a premier Presbyterian theologian, wrote, "No one, however rich his display of apparent Christian graces, is ever baptized on the basis of infallible knowledge that Christ dwells in him. All baptism is inevitably administered on the basis not of certain knowledge, but of presumption." [1]

5. When we study what the Bible teaches about the details of baptism, we derive more from inference and indirect reasoning than by direct Bible statements. Each side in the baptismal debate tends to act as if we have a definite edge in terms of Bible evidence. But we all deal with small clues and inferences in the biblical text to argue our cases. Growing up in the Baptist church, I heard preachers imply that since Jesus "went down into" the river and came "up out of" the river, that meant full immersion was the only right mode for baptism. Sorry folks, the literal text in this instance proves nothing about immersion. It only informs us that the place where Jesus was baptized was, in fact, the Jordan River. River depth was an open question. Did Jesus stand with John in ankle-deep Jordan River shallows as water was dipped and poured over him? Or were the two men in a shoulder-deep pool where immersion was natural and easy to perform? We do not know with certainty.

For much of its length, in contrast to mighty rivers in America, the Jordan River of today is barely a healthy creek. It might be compared with the Conestoga River near my home in Lancaster County, Pennsylvania. It is deep enough for us to canoe or kayak in it, but use of a motorboat is mostly out of the question. Many paintings and church frescoes produced by artists in the earliest Christian centuries depict John and Jesus standing in ankle-deep water, where immersion would be quite impossible, so John is shown pouring water over Jesus' head. (A huge canvas hanging in the Church of the Nativity at Bethlehem displayed this viewpoint upon my visit there in the year 2000.) Shall we consider these works of art to be authoritative images because of being painted closer to the 1st century? Truth is, whether Jesus' baptism occurred by immersion, dipping, or pouring of water is simply not stated in or concluded by Scripture. Dare I suggest that perhaps God left it this way as a matter of divine indifference?

We must always be careful not to presume more than the text of Scripture actually teaches. But when the Word of God does speak in clear affirmations, we must cling to facts. The Westminster Confession of Faith 1.6 wisely states, "The whole counsel of God concerning all things necessary...is either expressly set forth in Holy Scripture, or by good and necessary consequence may be deduced from Scripture." No side in baptism debates can entirely avoid relying upon some "good and necessary consequence" type arguments from the Word.

Chapter Three

The Covenant of Grace

IF YOU ARE TEMPTED to skip this chapter to get to material you think is more interesting, please don't. You might as well toss this book aside completely if you pull the plug on consideration of the covenant of grace. We must talk about this topic to lay the foundation for biblical baptism for the believer's child. So please be patient with me. Although I will rarely even mention the word baptism in this chapter, I promise you will eventually see the goal to which these doctrinal preliminaries lead.

The Bible's Spinal Column

Many corporations take pains to formulate mission statements in which they concisely define the company's overall task. Has God ever done anything similar? What was God's overarching purpose relating to human salvation through the entire Scriptures, Old Testament to New Testament?

Boiling the matter down, we find even in the early pages of Genesis that God was determined to rescue out of the mass of sinful humanity a people of faith to call his own – his covenant people. In all that the Lord did to save us through Jesus Christ, he was aiming to gather around Himself a people who would seek by faith to live out the reality of "be holy as I am holy."

First, the Lord dealt with Israel as his "Exhibit A" people. Then, increasingly from many other nations, the Lord God sought to gather to himself a spiritual commonwealth about whom He could say for all eternity, "I will be your God and you will be my people." This purpose forms the spinal column of Scripture, from Genesis to Revelation.

When Peter preached his epic Acts 2 Pentecost Day sermon that ignited fires of conversion for 3,000 souls in Jerusalem, he told a mostly Jewish crowd that they were responsible for killing the Messiah of Israel. Hearing Peter's accusation, the masses were deeply convicted and asked in real distress, "What shall we do?" Peter's famous answer in Acts 2:38 was, "Repent and be baptized every one of you in the name of Jesus Christ for the forgiveness of your sins, and you will receive the gift of the Holy Spirit."

If we hear these words filtered through our 21st-century American culture, we quickly assume Peter was simply calling individuals to trust in Christ as Savior, what many today call "praying the sinner's prayer." Indeed, Peter did call for that. But it is very important to realize that Peter added, without much of a pause, the words of Acts 2:39: "For the promise is for you and for *your children* and for all who are far off, everyone whom the Lord our God calls to himself."

Most of Peter's audience that day was made up of Israelites from many scattered lands, all in town for the Pentecostal holy days. These Jewish hearers knew implicitly that Peter spoke to them in covenant terminology. He was challenging heads of Israelite families to trust Jesus Christ as Lord themselves and also to lead their gathered households to the feet of Jesus as their true Messiah. This was exactly what heads of Jewish homes had sought to do for centuries because of God's frequently spoken covenant with them as a people called out to be separated from the unwashed, godless masses of mankind.

Early Roots of the Covenant of Grace

The covenant of grace appears in the Bible as early as God's saving acts toward Noah and his family. Because Noah trusted in the Lord and visibly obeyed him, the Lord set Noah's family apart and designed to rescue them from worldwide judgment by flood.

Few people notice the link that 1 Peter 3:20-21 makes between the waters of the worldwide deluge in Noah's day and New Testament baptism. Peter wrote, "a few, that is, eight persons, were brought safely through water. Baptism, *which corresponds to this*, now saves you, not as a removal of dirt from the body but as an appeal to God for a good conscience, through the resurrection of Jesus Christ...." Noah's experience was the first time God gave mankind a visible covenant sign – a rainbow – as his pledge of faithfulness in covenant relationship. Hold that thought. We shall see more about covenant signs shortly.

We find more formal statements about the covenant of grace in Genesis 15 and 17. Genesis 17:6-7 is a capsule summation, as the Lord tells Abraham, "I will make you exceedingly fruitful, and I will make you into nations, and kings shall come from you. And *I will establish my covenant* between me and you and your offspring after you throughout their generations for an everlasting covenant, to be God to you and to your offspring after you." Here again, the covenant is God's saving initiative to claim for himself a people of faith to walk with their God on earth and in eternity. Evangelical believers of our day are really referring to God's covenant of grace when they use the terminology "the plan of salvation."

Centuries ago, Reformed scholar Francis Turretin defined the covenant of grace as "a spiritual pact defined in Christ, entered into by the offended God as Initiator and offending sinners as respondents." In this sacred contract, God promised to forgive man freely on account of Christ, while man responds with faith and obedience.

The initial covenant was primarily made with Israel as a nation, yet many individual Israelites forsook the Lord, just as God had foreseen they would; it was no surprise to Him. From earliest Bible times, Old Testament prophecy indicated that the covenant promise was not exclusively for Israel. Other nations would also be blessed through the Jews, and in future days there would compose a spiritual "Israel" formed out of all nationalities who trusted the Lord and walked with Him by repentance and faith. So the covenant of grace even from earliest beginning was always intended to bring blessing to non-Jews who sought faith in God's appointed Messiah and Lord.

Galatians 3:8 states, "And the Scripture, foreseeing that God would justify the Gentiles by faith, preached the gospel beforehand to Abraham, saying, 'In you shall all the nations be blessed.'" In the whole Old Testament, God's covenant was like a "contract" with a vast people whom he sought after, calling them out from their various places in the world to obey and trust him, and thus to receive his salvation.

The Old Testament contains many covenant reaffirmations, as new generations needed reminders of God's calling. God's covenant was further confirmed through Moses in detailed laws given at Sinai. The Ten Commandments are simply covenant morality summarized. Later, the covenant was reiterated to David – with the idea God would always have a king from

David's line to rule his people. In Jeremiah 31:31, the Lord says that in future times he will write his covenant deep upon the hearts of his people and it will be called the "new" covenant. Jeremiah 32:38-40 summarizes, "And they shall be my people, and I will be their God. I will give them one heart and one way, that they may fear me forever, for their good and the good of their children after them. I will make with them an everlasting covenant, that I will not turn away from doing good to them." The so-called new covenant wasn't a brand-new creation. It was more a renewal of the covenant from Noah and Abraham's day, only with more emphasis on people of all nations as potential recipients.

This is a very brief tracing of a large concept. This simple plan for God to initiate and pursue the covenant of grace, forming a historic people in all ages to call his own, runs through the Bible like iron reinforcing rods through a concrete foundation.

Only One Way of Salvation

To change the metaphor, the development of the covenant runs like a scarlet thread of divine purpose through the entire Bible. We must remember that God was always doing just one thing in both the Old and New Testaments: forming a covenant people to exist for his praise. He was doing it in Israel of old, and he is doing it now in the universal church still being called out of all nations today.

From the very beginning, God's plan for the ages had salvation by way of the Cross of Jesus as its crowning stroke of fulfillment. The first prophecy of the Cross is uttered by God in Genesis 3:15 when God tells Satan in the Garden of Eden that the offspring of the woman will "bruise your head, and you shall bruise his heel."

The plan of the covenant of grace therefore unites the two testaments. Old Testament Israel and the "spiritual Israel" of the Christian church are really one people throughout history. The Lord was not working out Plan A for the Jews and Plan B for the rest of us who are non-Jews.

Jesus testifies as to the unity of the covenant in John 8:56 when he says, "Your father Abraham rejoiced that he would see my day. He saw it and was glad." Believers in older times looked forward to the Messiah, who they only very dimly realized would be Jesus Christ. We also trust in the same Savior, and we are united to Old Testament believers under one Lord. Galatians 3:29 declares, "And if you are Christ's, then you are Abraham's offspring, heirs according to promise (covenant)." A true Israelite, the Bible says, is any man or woman from Abraham's day forward to our 21st century who belongs by faith to the Covenant Redeemer, Jesus Christ. In a fascinating comment, Hebrews 11:26 says, "[Moses] considered the reproach of Christ greater wealth than the treasures of Egypt...." Do you hear that? Even in his ancient time, Moses looked to the same Lord of the covenant as you and I do, and his name was Jesus!

Many agree that we find a good summary statement of God's covenant of grace spanning the Old and New Testaments in Psalm 103:17,18: "But the steadfast love of the Lord is from everlasting to everlasting on those that fear Him, and his righteousness to children's children, to those who keep his covenant..."

Approaching God in Covenant Families

Now then, in earlier times for Israel, membership in a family mattered more than whatever nation one came from. Family was absolutely everything in Old Testament Israel. The Bible therefore teaches that God's normal pattern is to win hearts to himself as a male head of a covenant household leads his entire family in spiritual matters. In ancient Israel, the Lord intended fathers to lead their children in spiritual matters and husbands to lead their wives.

Be very clear on this issue: fathers could not believe on behalf of the children as their spiritual substitutes. The Old Testament has many examples of devout fathers whose children utterly forsook the Lord, and these offspring were not saved merely because of their parentage. Each generation and every individual ultimately gives his own account in matters of faith and morality before God. However, God ordained the covenant family to be the natural cradle for faith development.

Bearing in mind all that we have said about the covenant of grace up to this point, look again to Acts 2:38-39. Here we find Peter at the opening bell of the Christian church calling for people to "repent and be baptized every one of you in the name of Jesus Christ for the forgiveness of your sins..." Hardly pausing for breath, Peter then tells his nearly all-Jewish audience (which is listening with centuries of covenant-based filters in place), "For the promise (covenant) is for you and for your children and for all who are far off, everyone whom the Lord our God calls to himself."

Do you see? Peter surely did call for individuals to trust in Christ that day, challenging them to respond to the Lord in baptism as adult disciples. However, if the response Peter sought did not mean approaching God as a family, in which husbands and fathers should continue giving covenant leadership to entire households, then Peter surely had some explaining to do! Newly reborn Jewish Christians of the early church did not have in mind the same "every man for himself" evangelism that dominates the minds of today's American evangelicals. 1st-century Jewish Christians still assumed a corporate solidarity of their households in spiritual matters. Had Peter not meant what Jewish believers in Jesus had always understood – that God's covenant is with new believers in Christ as Lord and their children also – then his hearers would have been deeply confused. Since Peter did use covenant terminology in Acts 2:39, his hearers assumed that God still expected in this new gospel age that heads of families should continue to provide spiritual incubators where fathers act as spiritual leaders for their homes. In doing so, they would naturally include household members of all ages for baptism – as a new covenant sign.

Chapter Four

Signs of the Covenant, Old and New

LIKE CHILDREN, WE LEARN best with visual aids. So God has dealt kindly with us as he affirmed his covenant throughout biblical history. For instance, the entire bloody sacrificial system of the Old Testament acts like a graphic billboard, pounding home the lesson that every sin requires death. And I already mentioned the rainbow, an historic visual aid that confirmed God's promise to Noah.

Now we must talk about two more pictorial signs of the covenant: circumcision and the Passover Supper. The first began as a once and for all initiatory sign, obviously for males only. The second is intended for annual repetition, to be experienced by entire covenant families. Once we better understand the Scriptural purposes of these signs, we will return to the discussion of baptism.

Circumcision – The Initiatory Sign

In Genesis 17:10-11, the Lord shows Abraham, "Every male among you shall be circumcised....and it shall be a sign of the covenant between me and you." We have to admit that it seems downright odd for the Lord to choose this ritual of cutting away the unnecessary foreskin of the male's reproductive organ to be of such spiritual importance. Some find the subject embarrassing to talk about. Why should the surgical alteration of the penis of an eight-day-old baby boy be given such great emphasis in the Word of God?

With a little reflection, we may begin to see the Lord's reasoning was not so obscure after all. First, circumcision was a permanent mark inflicted on the body of all Israelite males. Since the husbands and fathers in this patriarchal society were charged to rule in their households, the Lord wanted his men of faith to be set apart from all other males in the world by placing a permanent scar of indisputable origin on their bodies. Circumcision represented an act of cleansing of the flesh by blood being shed.

Women were also included in the covenant blessings, but they were not regarded as independent spiritual agents. Women of that day were always under the authority of a father, a husband, or a brother, so they did not require a separate covenant sign.

God wanted his people to be separated and pure and to marry only within the boundaries of the covenant people. Since sexual liaisons were a primary occasion in which they might be tempted to depart from their faith, this surgical mark served as an unforgettable reminder to be "holy" or set apart to the Lord's direction for their entire lives. If an Israelite man had intimate relations with a non-Israelite woman, she would recognize the difference between his body versus all non-Israelite men.

So circumcision was how Old Testament men of faith were initiated into being "set apart" to the Lord. Much later, Romans 4:11 calls circumcision a sign and seal of faith. That does not mean it guaranteed that true faith in God already resided in the heart of every boy or man so marked. Circumcision was cut into the bodies of all Israelite boys long before it could be known what they would individually do in matters of faith in their promised redeemer.

The sign of circumcision preceded individual faith but pointed toward its intended realization. The eight-day-old boy being circumcised did not yet have conscious faith to choose the Lord. But he was dedicated to participating in a great heritage. He might later reject his heritage, as millions did. But if he trusted God, he would discover the great blessings that came from obedience and fearing the Lord.

Passover – The Annual Covenant Reminder

Exodus 12 tells us of the establishment of the Passover meal as the second major covenant sign. It is another visual object lesson for God's people to not only remember, but actually reenact his mercy in sparing them from the death of the firstborn while they were slaves in Egypt. Passover celebrated the way God let the Israelites plunder their Egyptian masters and reminded them how God freed them from slavery and preserved them through potential catastrophe in the Red Sea, crushing the pursuing chariots of their oppressors. Entire Israelite families were to be active in the Passover meal, as young children asked their fathers: "What do these things mean?" This was how covenant lessons and identity were passed on from generation to generation.

Just when you are beginning to think I have forgotten the main subject of this book, we find ourselves at a turning point. Now all our discussion about God's covenant finally comes to focus on the matter of baptism.

We are familiar with how the covenant of grace continues through the Cross and resurrection into the gospel age. The covenant of grace remains in place to define believers' relationship with God as his called people, separated from the world. But the signs of the covenant of grace have been transformed for the new age of the gospel of the Cross. The signs of the "new covenant" are no longer bloody – since the blood of Christ has been shed once for all time. Now we believe the Passover ritual gives way to the Lord's Supper and the sign of circumcision is replaced by baptism.

The Lord's Supper Replaces Passover

The point that the Lord's Supper replaces Passover is not difficult for us to accept. Matthew 26:17,19, and other gospel references show that it was the Passover meal which Jesus celebrated with his disciples the night before he died. In the midst of that supper, he turned its emphasis to himself. Of the bread he says, "Take, eat; this is my body" (Matthew. 26:26). And of the Passover cup he says, "Drink of it, all of you, for this is my blood of the covenant, which is poured out for many for the forgiveness of sins" (Matthew 26:27, 28). Few would dispute that Jesus consciously, deliberately transformed the covenant sign of Passover into a new covenant supper, celebrating his own presence as Lord of the covenant with his people of faith.

Baptism Replaces Circumcision

Although it is easy to see the parallel between Passover and Lord's Supper, it may be more difficult to persuade you that circumcision gives way to baptism in the age of the church. However, we do find the case for this in the New Testament – both stated and implied.

Today, the "circumcision" we ought to value is spiritual, not literal. Men and women alike must experience it. Listen to Romans 2:28-29: "For no one is a Jew who is merely one outwardly, nor is circumcision outward and physical. But a Jew is one inwardly, and circumcision is a matter of the heart, by the Spirit, not by the letter." Paul also parallels this thought in Philippians 3:3: "For we are the circumcision, who worship by the Spirit of God and glory in Christ Jesus and put no confidence in the flesh." Do you see? God still values the basic meaning of circumcision, but no longer as an outward ritual.

What God seeks today, as in earlier days, is a spiritual, internal surgery that cuts away the deadness and dullness of our unbelief. In Deuteronomy 10:16, Moses is God's mouthpiece to tell Israel, "Circumcise therefore the foreskin of your heart, and be no longer stubborn." Deuteronomy 30:6 tells the people that the Lord himself will do the needed soul surgery: "And the Lord your God will circumcise your heart and the heart of your offspring, so that you will love the Lord your God with all your heart and with all your soul, that you may live."

A Crucial Link: Colossians 2:11 & 12

You may ask: Is there any biblical text directly linking baptism as the New Testament replacement for circumcision? Yes. Read Colossians 2:11-12, in which the apostle says, "In [Christ] also you were circumcised with a circumcision made without hands, by putting off the body of the flesh, by the circumcision of Christ, having been buried with him in baptism, in which you were also raised with him through faith in the powerful working of God, who raised him from the dead." My trust in the atonement of Christ cancelled my slave-obligation to sin. My redemption price was paid in the death of Jesus; I am ransomed and released from the dictatorship of Satan.

Paul explains quite clearly in Colossians 2 that water baptism is symbolic of internal circumcision of the believing heart. Baptism symbolizes the death of our sin nature, just as circumcision once did. In neither case should we cling to a merely external physical act. Baptism is God's testimony to what only he can accomplish by forgiving a believing heart of sin for the sake of Christ.

This brings us full circle on the issue of the covenant. We now see that Presbyterian and Reformed people use the same rationale in arguing for the value of baptizing a believer's child as the Old Testament once argued for Israelite boys to be circumcised. Remember, the Israelite boy was circumcised in infancy; his cooperation in receiving this bloody covenant sign was neither asked for nor expected. The key issue was not that an infant intelligently confirmed his faith via circumcision, but that God was announcing the covenant.

The covenant sign was about initiation into the people of God long before this could be comprehended by the recipient. Even Abraham received the covenant sign of circumcision before he had the fullness of faith in the Lord. God further commanded that Isaac and all future sons born in Israel would receive circumcision just days after their birth. Only later, as adults, would they understand what it was all about, and hopefully take ownership of God's covenant promises – all of which pointed their hopes to a future Messiah, the Lord Jesus Christ.

We have seen that, once circumcised, the young Israelite boy would be expected to confirm his faith and a calling to personal holiness as he grew to maturity. Parallel to this, the sign of baptism welcomes male and female children of New Covenant believers into the household of faith – in hopeful expectation that their walk with the Lord as disciples will be confirmed later on.

Dr. R. C. Sproul once summarized the matter in this way: "In the Old Testament God ordered a sign of faith to be applied even before personal faith was present. Since that was clearly done, it is erroneous to argue that a corresponding sign of faith cannot be administered today before the believer's child shows faith." [2]

Chapter Five

Additional Evidences

WE'VE SPENT THE LAST two chapters looking at Scripture to make our argument supporting baptism of the believer's child. We developed the analogy of God's covenant, the covenant of grace, and relations between old and new covenant signs.

Now we move forward to points defending baptism for the believer's child, drawn primarily from the historical and cultural side of things.

New Testament Household Baptisms

The New Testament presents just twelve specific cases of baptisms done for named individuals. Three of these, one-fourth of the total number, involve "household" baptisms. We must be careful to not try to prove too much from this fact. But likewise, this evidence should not be ignored, since household baptisms happened within the lifetimes of the original apostles, and some were actually administered under direct apostolic supervision.

If Peter or other 1st-century apostles had intended for Jewish-born believers in Christ to radically depart from their assumption that covenant signs include the whole family, wouldn't we expect to see some definite instruction about that? If the Baptistic case for immersion of only adult believers is correct, we might expect to find many more examples clarifying that change.

Let's look at the two household baptisms that occurred in Philippi. Paul's eventful missionary journey there led to the establishment of a local church which became dear to his heart. In Acts 16:14, we learn of Lydia, a merchant woman of Philippi who dealt in textiles. "The Lord opened her heart to pay attention to what was said by Paul." As an immediate result, she and the members of her household were baptized.

Also, when Paul and Silas were held in the jail at Philippi, Acts 16:33-34 tells of the aftermath of an earthquake at midnight. They and all the other prisoners remained in place. Seeing something totally remarkable about the faith of these men, the amazed jailer inquires, "What must I do to be saved?" (30). The result was, "and he was baptized at once, he and all his family" (33).

How much can we claim to know about these two Philippian households? This much is reasonable to conclude: first, both were substantial homes of persons who were community leaders. Both Lydia the cloth merchant and the unnamed jailer were Roman citizens of some community stature. Their households were most likely middle- to upper-middle class establishments, with a high likelihood that servants were housed therein. According to standards of the day, such a house might also have included multiple generations of the core family, with grandparents, parents, and young children all living under the same roof.

Though we cannot be precise about who was included within these two homes, in both cases multiple persons of varying ages were included in the sign of faith applied by baptism at the instigation of a family leader who first showed faith in Christ. Do we know if there were infants involved? No, we do not. We cannot say either way with certainty. However, it seems a greater logical stretch to believe no children at all were included.

A third household baptism is mentioned in 1 Corinthians 1:16, where Paul notes only in passing that he baptized the household of Stephanas. Although little can be deduced from such a toss-off remark, the mere fact that Paul mentions it so casually shows that he regards it as unremarkable for multiple members of a household to be baptized together in a New Testament church. It appears the practice was so common that it did not warrant any special defense.

The vital issue in view here is a New Testament continuation of the Old Testament covenant household principle. The head of the home acted as a leader in spiritual decisions made on behalf of the entire household.

Uniform Practice of Christians for Many Centuries

When I was a Baptist in my teenage years, I accepted on faith the Baptist position on how infant baptism came about in the unfolding of church history. I was taught that believers-only baptism by immersion was the "normal" New Testament practice until, at some uncertain date, doctrinal corruption crept in, and people began baptizing infants as a breakdown of the purer believers-only baptismal practice of early days.

Over the years, I have heard Baptists explain church history in just that way. However, that really does not conform to historical fact. Examining church history, we find a high probability that infant children of believers were baptized as a matter of course from early New Testament days onward, with no sudden change of practice discoverable at any point.

Prior to about 180 AD, there is an odd silence in early church records about modes of baptismal practice. The earliest church fathers apparently did not see this as a subject requiring much comment. But in 180 AD, the theologian Origen testified that he was baptized as an infant, near to his birth, which would have been only one generation removed from the day of Pentecost. In An Epistle to the Romans, Origen states flatly, "Infant baptism was the practice of the apostles."

Irenaeus of Lyon, who died in 202 AD, testifies that it was normal for infant baptism to be practiced alongside believer's baptism for adult converts. Cyprian, bishop of Carthage, born around 200 AD, argued strongly in favor of infant baptism. None of these early witnesses looked upon infant baptism for a child of believers as being a novelty introduced after the original apostles died.

Unfortunately, we cannot say that all supporters of infant baptism in those early centuries practiced it based on covenant principles alone. It must be admitted that some early advocates did mistakenly regard covenant baptism of young children as a saving sacrament, endorsing baptismal regeneration and all its accompanying superstitions that contradict biblical salvation by grace alone. Covenantal arguments supporting infant baptism may have become obscured for some church leaders in those earliest days. In other words, for centuries Christians correctly brought their children for baptism, even though many had either forgotten, or never knew, sound biblical reasons for doing so.

Tertullian was a 3rd-century theologian who opposed infant baptism, but he did so in a qualified way. While he did not absolutely forbid it, he felt it was preferable to wait until the child could profess faith. However, it is a monumental fact that, aside from isolated voices like Tertullian, there was no widespread outcry against the practice of infant baptism for nearly fifteen centuries.

Other than a few individual voices here and there, no large-scale dissent against baptizing believers' children was heard in Christian ranks until the Anabaptists attacked the practice in the 16th-century Reformation. One Mennonite leader called the practice "a senseless, blasphemous abomination, contrary to all Scripture." However, most mainstream continental Protestant Reformers, including Luther and Calvin, solidly defended the practice upon covenant grounds.

I acknowledge that by the classic rules of logic, any "argument from silence" is classified as logically weak. However, silence in place of the huge theological dissent we might have expected to arise in the early church is remarkable.

If infant baptism was indeed contrary to the original practice in the lifetime of the apostles, then it is legitimate for us to wonder why no uproar of dispute accompanied a supposed departure by the 1st- and 2nd-century body of Christians into a "wrong" practice.

There was no outcry simply because there never was such a marked departure.

God's Tender Mercy for Children

How does God regard children? Does Scripture teach that children have a unique regard in the mind and heart of the Lord? We must tread carefully here so we don't descend into sappy sentimentalism and disregard the Bible's teaching on original sin simply because infants and children seem cute and innocent. We must not and cannot ignore the sober fact that we all are spiritually "dead in trespasses and sins" from the moment of our birth onward.

A quick story from Dr. John Gerstner, a 20th-century Presbyterian seminary professor, makes this point well. Gerstner had a razor sharp, logical mind and, while he was a friendly man, it could also be said that he did not "suffer fools gladly." I once heard Dr. Gerstner describe a Sunday when he was filling the pulpit as a substitute for a vacationing pastor. As he arrived at the church, an elder informed him that there was to be an infant baptism that day. He then briefed Dr. Gerstner on a unique procedure that this congregation's resident minister followed: a long-stemmed white rose was to be dipped in the baptistry, then the water from the rose was to be sprinkled upon the child's head.

When Dr. Gerstner coyly asked if there was symbolic meaning intended in this rather odd practice, the elder replied, "Why I guess it is meant to symbolize the sinless purity of the infant." (The fish had now taken the bait.)

Dr. Gerstner asked, "Then what does baptism represent?" The elder said, "Well, I guess Christ's washing of sins." Next came Dr. Gerstner's finishing stroke: "Then please tell me which baby am I going to baptize today, one who is already pure from his sins? Or one who needs a Savior just as you and I do?" Needless to say, the foolishly placed white rose was not used in the infant baptism on that Sunday morning.

As we have said, we must avoid the sentimentalism that assumes children are pure in heart apart from redemption accomplished by Christ. Not true! Even a one-hour-old infant is Adam's descendant and needs Christ to act as his Savior. So, knowing that children need gospel salvation as much as adults do, we ask: Does Scripture regard salvation for younger children to be received in any unique manner other than by their conscious step of faith in Christ?

One day, Jesus called a very young child to his side and said, "Truly, I say to you, unless you turn and become like children, you will never enter the kingdom of heaven. Whoever humbles himself like this child is the greatest in the kingdom of heaven" (Matthew 18:3-5). Unquestionably, the main lesson of that text is that Jesus viewed a young child as the epitome of dependency and pure trust toward adults. Children are eager to please and quick to express love; they are generally easily taught and molded. Jesus pointed to these attributes of childlike character as a model for how Christian disciples should relate to their Heavenly Father.

But does not the passage tell us about how the Lord regards children in general, as infants with their own eternal souls? I have been helped in this matter by writings of Dr. John MacArthur (ironically, a staunch Baptist author backing me up on this point). Commenting on Matthew 18, MacArthur says that the analogy Jesus uses here must be rooted in actual truth. That is, unless flesh and blood young children who die were as a class already accepted into the kingdom of heaven as saved persons, they would be poor models for Jesus to hold up for behavioral imitation by adult disciples.

Other biblical indicators also suggest that God requires a different level of spiritual and moral accountability from children who die before attaining an age of intellectual and moral discernment than he requires from adults. In Jonah 4:11, the Lord urges Jonah to pity the pagan people in Nineveh who need to find saving repentance. The Lord then adds in a call for Jonah to become his prophet to that city, to "Nineveh, that great city, in which there are more than 120,000 persons who do not know their right hand from their left...." Who are these people? We presume many or most of this mass of 120,000 souls were Ninevite children. Similarly, Jeremiah 19:4 refers to children sacrificed unto the false god Baal as "the blood of innocents." And in yet another place, Deuteronomy 1:39, the Lord is referring to young children when he tells

Moses, "Your children, who today have no knowledge of good or evil, they shall go in there (the promised land)."

From such evidence, it appears that the Lord draws a line of mercy in favor of children who cannot yet make rational decisions about sinning, repenting, or believing in Christ as God and Savior. To address this issue some theologians hold to the existence of "an age of spiritual accountability." It is true that no one knows precisely at what age within the mercy of God a line of accountability for the expression of saving faith in Jesus might be drawn. And the age would differ from child to child.

Into this broad category of special cases (enfolding into salvation actual infants who are under the grace of God apart from a mature act of faith), we may include souls who are mentally deficient. Remaining very much as children, they will never attain full moral cognition or spiritual discernment in their entire lifetimes. What happens to any human soul if they die before they are able to trust Christ? Would we say that still-born or aborted infants, or for that matter any child who dies in infancy, or those with mental handicaps, are barred from inclusion in God's saving grace? We must ultimately leave this question to God's sovereign government. However, one classic Bible hint toward an answer is seen in 2 Samuel 12:23. Upon hearing that the newborn son of David and Bathsheba has died, mournful David says, "Can I bring him back again? I shall go to him, but he will not return to me." We interpret his utterance to say that this particular infant child of a man of faith was already in heaven. Thus David, acting as God's prophetic spokesman, was confident of meeting his already-dead infant son in eternity.

Based on what little evidence we do have, it has long been assumed that believers' children who die at a young age are considered to be among the elect and are received into glory by God's special mercy, even though they cannot exercise personal faith. We have the joint wisdom of several dozen Puritan divines writing about this subject in the Westminster Confession 10.3 in these words: "Elect infants, dying in infancy, are regenerated and saved by Christ through the Spirit, who works when, where and how he pleases. So also are all other elect persons who are incapable of being outwardly called by the ministry of the Word."

Do you see? We are not denying that infants are born into the curse of Adam's sin. They do need a savior as surely as they were born into the human condition as a sinner in this world. Surely it is true that only redemption as offered in Christ can save them. However, we also believe God in sovereign mercy may apply that saving grace of the Cross wherever he wills, even apart from rational expressions of faith, in what we may call the "special circumstance" of a young child or mentally incompetent person.

The question gets harder to answer if it is pushed to the next level: Does this mean all children who die before they could pass a "faith IQ test," and all mentally incompetent persons in the world should be considered automatically elect, regardless of Christ-centered faith held by their parents? Would this include 100 percent of all aborted children, millions of whom are cut off from drawing their first breath every year in America? And does it include all children of Hindu, Muslim, and pagan parents? We begin to realize that the implications of these questions are huge. Unfortunately the Bible does not give us black and white solutions. We walk by faith here, not by sight.

For any who want to read further on this subject, I strongly recommend a little book by John MacArthur titled Safe in the Arms of God (Thomas Nelson Publishers, 2003). In it, MacArthur speaks about his own concurrence with John Newton, who was a careful Bible scholar as well as a hymn writer. Newton said, "I cannot be sorry for the death of infants. How many storms do they escape! Nor can I doubt in my private judgment that they are included in the election of grace." Notice, Newton said this was his "private judgment." I think he was admitting the biblical evidence for the conclusion is not as fully revealed as he might have wished it could be.

To add one more bit of evidence, in Matthew 18:10, Jesus says, "See that you do not despise one of these little ones. For I tell you that in heaven their angels always see the face of my Father who is in heaven." Then in verse 14, he continues, "...it is not the will of my Father who is in heaven that one of these little ones should perish." The Greek word for "little ones" in this context most likely includes all truly regenerated and justified Christians of any age since all of us must become profoundly childlike to become a true disciple. You must become a "little one" yourself to be a Christian.

This last section has admittedly moved a bit beyond the subject of infant baptism proper. But one thing our hearts should affirm as each believer's child is baptized in a worship service is our hope that, if that child should die before reaching the ability to exercise rational faith in Christ, the Lord would certainly take this little one to himself – washed in the merits of Jesus at the Cross.

Chapter Six

What is Unique about a Believer's Covenant Child?

NOW THAT WE HAVE established the biblical principle of representative headship by the spiritual head of a covenant family, let's think about how to apply it in our homes today.

In Acts 16:30, the Philippian jailer asks, "Sirs, what must I do to be saved?" Paul's reply tells him what he and others could do: "Believe in the Lord Jesus, and you will be saved, you and your household." We cannot rightly conclude that all other adults in the household automatically came to faith just because the jailer did so. No such guarantee could ever be given in light of the gospel message in the New Testament. Yet we see here that faith in Christ shown by the head of the home did at least lead to covenant baptism for all in that household unit.

1 Corinthians 7:14

In first Corinthians 7, we find another instructive passage from Paul, this one not being about baptism at all. Instead, it speaks to the question of unequally yoked marriages. Should a believer in Christ remain married to a spouse who is not a Christian? Paul urges that under no circumstance should there be casual divorce in this situation. The general principle is that "the wife should not separate from her husband..." and "...the husband should not divorce his wife" (10-11).

The apostle reminds the Corinthians that the living Holy Spirit is resident and working within that mixed marriage via the believing spouse. Therefore the power of the Spirit to influence the unbelieving partner should never be discounted. It leads Paul to this conclusion: "For the unbelieving husband is made holy because of his wife, and the unbelieving wife is made holy because of her husband. Otherwise your children would be unclean, but as it is, they are holy" (14).

In this context, the word "holy," or "sanctified" as some translations have it, could not possibly mean saved in the full gospel sense of being eternally justified by God's grace through faith. For any person or object to be holy or sanctified in the primary definition means set apart from a mere worldly purpose; consecrated to God. Saying the believer's child is holy indicates that he is in a privileged position. He dwells close to the kingdom of God, under its constant influence, because at least one parent as a vessel of the Spirit is intently molding that child's entire development with kingdom attitudes and actions. Therefore this blessed child lives at the very threshold of the entry to Christ's kingdom. Paul is promising that the word and life examples of parental godliness will exert a regulative influence upon that young life.

For such a child, it will potentially be a rather small step from his set-apart position to one day cross the threshold to embrace Christ fully with heart and will. Over the years, I have heard numerous children from Christian homes recount their personal testimony with words like these: "I never can recall a time when I did not love Christ and revere Him as my Lord." Is that not a wonderful testimony? Saving faith remains God's individual gift to a covenant child by the Holy Spirit, but the gift often opens gradually in life, without a sudden jolt. It may proceed by quiet baby steps of grace at work by the Holy Spirit in a home where parental influence is steadily applied and accepted without resistance.

Thus we say any child with a Christian mother and/or father deserves to be under the sign of covenant baptism. For them, baptism announces God's forgiving grace available to wash away sin. Baptismal water is God's visible pledge to reward all who come to Him by way of repentance and faith in Christ. The covenant child is dedicated in hope that his set-apart position will bring him into full redemption in God's good timing. This is how circumcision functioned in the Old Testament home. So also today, we baptize the believer's child not out of sweet emotional sentiment, but because the practice squares with the Bible's own presentation of the covenant of grace.

Christ's Engagement Ring

When a young woman appears with a diamond ring on the third finger of her left hand, everyone knows what it means: she is newly engaged to be married. I have kidded some young ladies I have known, that for a few weeks they go about with their left hands raised in a somewhat unnatural position so all their friends can see the ring and happily exclaim about it with them. That shared joy is about much more than just a new piece of jewelry. We can truly say that a young woman's giddy excitement is about a covenant sign. For that's exactly what an engagement ring is. A man has told this woman: "I pledge to make you my wife. I single you out from all other women and promise to you my exclusive faithfulness to become to you a loving husband for our lifetimes. So here, in token of this pledge, I give you this diamond ring."

It is not far off the mark to call the baptism of a believer's child the engagement ring of Christ Jesus. It amounts to God's own declaration to become the Bridegroom of his elect covenant people. Baptism is about God pledging himself to us first and foremost, even before our responsive pledge of faith in him; before conscious acceptance by us of a redemption wrought for us in history by the cross and resurrection of Jesus Christ.

One flaw in my engagement ring analogy is that a human bridegroom can break his engagement pledge. As a sinner, he could prove unfaithful before or after completing his marital vow. So could the human bride, for that matter. However, Jesus Christ cannot and will not do this. The covenant promise affirmed in baptism for the believer's child cannot be broken by our Savior. The only question is, will the "bride" answer the Bridegroom's covenantal call?

Presumed to Be Elect?

Some people in the Presbyterian and Reformed camp speak about the position of the baptized child of believing parents in terms of what I call "presumptive election." They say that we ought to regard such children as being among God's elect until they clearly give some negative sign later in life that they are not the Lord's. Such famous and highly respected theologians as Charles Hodge and B.B. Warfield appear to have taken this viewpoint in the 19th century. [3]

I stand more in the mainstream, siding with those who teach that presuming that our baptized children definitely are elect may be a dangerous idea. It seems to go a step further than Scripture affirms. If we take our children's eternal security absolutely for granted before hearing and seeing verbal and character evidence of conversion, we might fail to pray for their souls as we ought to or neglect them as objects for evangelistic and moral nurture within our own homes.

Many examples from Bible history show us that bad spiritual fruit can grow from a good tree. Aaron's two sons were unfaithful as priests and lost their lives; David gave birth to rebellious Absalom. There are no foregone, final conclusions about any individual's standing in Christ apart from a lively testimony to the power of the Cross and visible works eventually kindled into a steady flame of faith. Children in Christian homes do enjoy wonderful advantages. Yet wise prudence requires us to treat baptized children as subjects for evangelistic witness. There should be systematic Bible nurturing and earnest prayers uplifted to heaven from our child's birth onward, until parents have that great joy of hearing the next generation confirm the covenant of grace in their own words and actions.

The Tremendous Potential of a Christian Home

My wife and I are proud parents of a daughter and three sons. Our children were raised in a pastor's home. They were always in church, the Bible was read to them at home, and we prayed both with and for them constantly. I bless God that now, as adults, all four of our children profess Jesus as their Lord and their lives appear to validate that testimony. Two of my sons have been ordained to serve as ruling elders. We have fifteen grandchildren (so far). For their apparently saved and sanctified lives, I am deeply grateful before God. Their redemption is all of grace, no doing of mine or my wife's.

If you asked my four children to recount their own testimonies, I believe each would tell some version of what I have sometimes labeled a "boring" conversion story. They had no life of extended debauchery and no Damascus Road flash crisis. In each case, they came to faith by gradual turnings in the road, developing spiritually within a safe family hothouse atmosphere of faith. I think they would say that they can hardly remember ever being outside the fold of Christ. I regard such a testimony as much to be desired – what we hope to hear from any covenant child. It is also our prayer for our grandchildren whom I have been privileged to baptize in that covenant sign.

God said of Abraham, the first biblical father to apply the sign of the covenant to his child, "For I have chosen him, that he may command his children and his household after him to keep the way of the Lord" (Genesis 18:19). The prime sphere of influence God uses to bring people to faith is their family or close friends.

My own father came from a religious but rather legalistic home. He was always a self-consciously moral man of good character and a Boy Scout troop leader when I was quite young. However, when I was 12 years old, I saw my father put his trust in Jesus. Suddenly the Bible and prayer were as much a part of our daily dinner table as dessert. Dad became a zealous witness for Christ and a selfless volunteer in many church endeavors. What this very visible turnabout by my own father meant to me was that, even if I were someday inclined to reject Christianity, I would have had a hard time getting past the sterling authenticity of my father's utterly transformed life.

We see this principle beautifully illustrated in Daniel Defoe's epic novel Robinson Crusoe. The book is one of my all-time favorites; I have re-read it many times. Here was a truly solitary man who did not hear another human voice on his remote island for many years. You may recall that Crusoe experienced a crisis of great sickness in which he nearly died. Severe illness and the prospect of death caused the solitary man to repent for the folly of his early life, when he had rejected the church and the counsel of a Christian home. Having run away to sea, he had lived a wild sailor's life, often cursing God. But then one day in his lonely island cave, with an open Bible in hand, the sick man cried out to God to save him by the merits of Jesus Christ. It was clear that both the power of God's Word and his memories of past nurture in a Christian home were God's saving instruments in the transformation of Robinson Crusoe's soul.

Here is the instruction the Lord gave to his covenant people in Deuteronomy 6:6-9: "And these words that I command you today shall be upon your heart. You shall teach them diligently to your children, and shall talk of them when you sit in your house and when you walk by the way, and when you lie down, and when you rise. You shall bind them as a sign on your hand, and they shall be as frontlets between your eyes. You shall write them on the doorposts of your house and on your gates."

Parents, you probably will not spare your child any good thing you can reasonably afford to do for them. You willingly buy them a good computer and fashionable clothes, pay membership fees for sports teams and college tuition. But, dare I ask, how are you investing for them in things that are eternal? Do you realize you will have largely won or lost the campaign for the character of your child by the time they are in first grade? The "wet cement" of their moral fiber and spiritual foundation begins to set terribly soon.

If you are a parent, do not trifle with baptism for your covenant child. Do not put it off saying, "I will wait, so my son can be baptized as a young teenager when he joins the church. Then he will have made up his own mind and it will be more meaningful to him that way...." I may be stepping on toes here, but that is unbiblical reasoning.

Covenant baptism symbolizes the greatest power in the universe – the supernatural strength of God the Holy Spirit to transform our children's lives in the image of Christ. God offers our children the engagement ring of Christ. Jesus who died and rose for us will not fail to be the faithful Bridegroom for all souls the heavenly Father has elected to give to Him. In water baptism we have a wonderful sacrament that proclaims his faithfulness to all generations.

Chapter Seven

Can We Have Peace About Baptism?

WHAT FOLLOWS IS AN imaginary conversation. Though built upon biblical incidents, surely this conversation never actually took place. But it could have...

In John 9 and Luke 18, Jesus heals two different unnamed men. Let's call the fellow from John 9, "Jerry." To heal Jerry's blindness, Jesus spits upon the dust and uses the resulting clay as a salve to put on the blind man's eyes. Jesus then tells him to go wash in a pool, after which Jerry sees things for the first time.

The man from Luke 18 is a blind beggar who we will name "Larry." This time Jesus uses no mud, but simply prays for Larry and speaks effective words that restore his sight.

Now, just suppose that these two fellows one day meet in the streets of Jerusalem. Upon comparing notes, they realize they were both given their sight by the same healer, Jesus. Larry exclaims, "Yes, that Jesus is some wonder worker. All he had to do was to pray and say to me, 'Your faith has healed you,' and immediately I could see again."

But Jerry says, "No, wait, my friend, I have to correct you. Your memory of how Jesus heals blindness is quite mistaken. You left out the part where he spat upon the mud and spread it on your eyes and then he charged you to go wash it off in the Pool of Siloam—"

Larry interrupts, "I don't know what you are talking about. That sounds pretty disgusting. I cannot think why a powerful healer like Jesus would mess around with mud on people's eyes!"

By now Jerry is getting angry. "Look, friend. I know from personal experience that Jesus heals eyes with mud only. If you did not have the holy mud applied to you, then I begin to doubt whether you can see anything clearly at all!"

Soon, the controversy escalates to the next level so that, in their frustration, the men stop speaking to each other. Before long each man gathers enough friends around himself to have two Christian congregations dedicated to healing services. Jerry leads the "Mudite" faction that starts a business selling bottled clay as an eye salve. Larry becomes bishop of the "Anti-Mudites" who encourage prayer to Jesus only for healing of blindness.

Pretty silly, right? Yet if we substitute modes of healing with modes of administering baptism in this fictional tale, you will realize I am not far from accurately depicting a centuries-old tragedy still being repeated in the Christian world today.

A Plea for Tolerance

We should never befriend the modern ecumenical spirit that calls for peace at any price. We cannot agree to the watering down of any essential Christian doctrine in the sole interest of getting along with heretics. However, it is vital to distinguish between what is essential doctrine that determines whether we can have fellowship in Christ, versus what is mere secondary opinion and not vital to saving faith.

In the sanctuary where I preach, a three-sided balcony is held up by eight large structural columns. I have told our congregation to think of those columns as if they were imperative doctrines like the deity of Christ, the inerrancy of Scripture, justification by faith, the bodily resurrection, and so on. Any compromise on those major points, and our church would fall. I would take up the sword and die for any of those doctrines. However, the practices and specific understanding of baptism are not structural columns. These are matters of secondary understanding about which we should be able to humbly disagree without fracturing Christian fellowship with true brothers and sisters.

So, can we learn to be charitable to one another regarding baptism?

There are aspects of both the covenant baptism view I have defended here and the baptistic idea of immersion baptism for believers that lack the full conclusiveness each view might wish for. Both sides must rely upon inference, example, and indirect proofs to make their cases from Scripture. A good dose of humility is needed by all parties, something that we as biblical believers are not always so good at modeling.

Ephesians 4:5: One Baptism

In Ephesians 4:3-6, Paul memorably calls believers to unity as he says, "[Be] eager to maintain the unity of the Spirit in the bond of peace. There is one body and one Spirit – just as you were called to the one hope that belongs to your call – one Lord, one faith, one baptism; one God and Father of all, who is over all and through all and in all."

I suggest that Paul is not even speaking in verse 5 about the various modes and practices surrounding water baptism. Instead, he prizes the baptism of the Holy Spirit, by whom we are incorporated into Christ in the first place. Baptism in the Spirit is an invisible, internal issue which does not involve water. Every Christian is baptized by the Holy Spirit when we are born again. Romans 8:9 insists that if we do not have the Holy Spirit, we do not have Christ.

In Ephesians: An Expositional Commentary, James Boice pinpoints the matter: "Have you been baptized into Christ? I do not care how you were baptized. I do not care whether it was in a church baptistry or a stream; whether with a little bit or a lot of water. Have you been publicly identified with Christ? That is the issue." [4]

Paul reminds us that there is only one virgin-born Son of God, one gospel, one historic Cross, one resurrection from the dead, and one eternal life. Only one Holy Spirit shatters deadness in our trespasses and sins and brings us alive in Christ. Therefore certainly only baptism in the living Holy Spirit is the true uniting power for the church of our great Savior.

An Obstacle to the Cross?

In 1 Corinthians 1:11-17, Paul chides the Corinthians about fractures in their Christian fellowship. One item causing irritation was bragging rights as to who had baptized each person. "Or were you baptized in the name of Paul? I thank God that I baptized none of you except Crispus and Gaius, so that no one may say that you were baptized in my name... For Christ did not send me to baptize but to preach the gospel, and not with words of eloquent wisdom, lest the cross of Christ be emptied of its power."

Paul is not saying here that water baptism is of no account. But he is clear-eyed in realizing how even a legitimate faith experience like baptism can be so pushed to the forefront that it obscures the preeminent Cross of Calvary. Even sacraments of the church can eclipse the gospel. Therefore, if I must, I will burn my baptismal certificate if it prevents me from looking into the face of my dear Savior and saying, "Nothing in my hand I bring, simply to thy Cross I cling!"

Dr. Francis Schaeffer was a minister in my denomination, the Presbyterian Church in America. He wrote a small, broad-spirited booklet on the subject of baptism. Schaeffer said, "No one has to accept our view of baptism to join our churches.... We should not ride our view of baptism as a hobby-horse any more than any other teaching. It is not the center of our theology, but neither should we fail to teach it in its proper place." [5]

Schaeffer captured the balanced spirit we seek. People who have been baptized in the name of the Trinity in the past will not be asked to be re-baptized to join our local churches. Our overriding concern in examining people for church membership is this: What has the power of the Cross accomplished in you? Do you profess faith in Jesus as the one and only Lord of the universe by the grace of God? Is the Spirit of Christ stirring in your life today, to convict you of sin and build you up in the truth of Scripture?

Let us always strive for the honor of Christ and thereby always endeavor to keep the main thing as the main thing!

Soli Deo Gloria.

Chapter Eight

Baptism as Taught in Reformed Creeds

WE CANNOT IMPROVE UPON doctrinal definitions forged after the Protestant Reformation in classic creeds that have long endured. I reproduce these portions of such creeds here without commentary, as the words speak powerfully in their own right. Let us review these summaries of biblical teaching on the meaning of our sacraments.

The Westminster Confession of Faith (1646)

Chapter 27.1 Sacraments are holy signs and seals of the covenant of grace. They were directly instituted by God to represent Christ and his benefits and to confirm our relationship to him. They are also intended to make a visual distinction between those who belong to the church and the rest of the world, and to solemnly bind

Christians to the service of God in Christ, according to his Word.

Chapter 27.3 The grace which is exhibited in or by the sacraments, rightly used, is not conferred by any power in them. Neither does the efficacy of a sacrament depend on the piety or intention of him who administers it, but rather on the work of the Spirit and on the word of institution, which contains...a promise of benefit to worthy receivers.

Chapter 27.4 There are only two sacraments ordained by Christ our Lord in the gospel: baptism and the Lord's Supper. Neither sacrament may be administered by any person except a minister of the Word, lawfully ordained.

Chapter 27.5 With regard to the spiritual realities signified and exhibited, the sacraments of the Old Testament were essentially the same as those of the New Testament.

Chapter 28.1 Baptism is a sacrament of the New Testament, ordained by Jesus Christ, by which the person baptized is solemnly admitted to the visible church. Baptism is also for him a sign and seal of the covenant of grace, of his ingrafting into Christ, of regeneration, of forgiveness of sins and of his surrender to God through Jesus Christ to walk in newness of life. By Christ's appointment, this sacrament is to be continued in the church until the end of the age.

Chapter 28.2 The outward element to be used in this sacrament is water, with which the person is to be baptized in the name of the Father, of the Son and of the Holy Spirit. Baptism is to be performed by a minister of the gospel, lawfully called to that office.

Chapter 28.3 Dipping of the person into the water is not necessary. Baptism is rightly administered by pouring or sprinkling water upon the person.

Chapter 28.4 Not only those who personally profess faith in and obedience to Christ, but also the infants of one or both believing parents are to be baptized.

Chapter 28.5 Although it is a great sin to despise or neglect this ordinance, nevertheless grace and salvation are not so inseparably connected with it that a person cannot be regenerated or saved without it. Neither is it true that all who are baptized are undoubtedly regenerated.

Chapter 28.6 The efficacy of baptism is not tied to the moment of time when it is administered. Nevertheless, by the right use of this ordinance the grace promised is not only offered but really is exhibited and conferred by the Holy Spirit to all (whether infants or adults) to whom that grace belongs, according to the counsel of God's own will and in his own time.

Chapter 28.7 The sacrament of baptism is to be administered only once to any person.

The Heidelberg Catechism (1563)

Question 74: Should infants too, be baptized?

Answer: Yes. For they as well as adults belong to God's covenant and community (Gen. 17:7) and no less than adults are promised forgiveness for sin through Christ's blood (Matt. 19:14) and the Holy Spirit who produces faith (Ps. 22:10, Isa. 44:1-3, Lk. 1:15, Acts 2:39, 16:31). Therefore they too, ought to be incorporated into the Christian church through baptism, the sign of the covenant and distinguished from the children of unbelievers (Acts 10:47, 1 Cor. 7:14). This was done in the Old Testament by circumcision (Gen. 17:9-14) in whose place baptism was instituted in the New Testament (Col. 2:11-13).

Vows for a Believer's Baptism in the PCA

(These are the Presbyterian Church in America membership questions, from Book of Church Order 57-5)

1. Do you acknowledge yourself to be a sinner in the sight of God, justly deserving his displeasure, and without hope, save in his sovereign mercy?

2. Do you believe in the Lord Jesus Christ as the Son of God and Savior of sinners, and do you receive and rest in him alone as he is offered to you in the Gospel?

3. Do you now resolve and promise in humble reliance on the grace of the Holy Spirit, that you will live as becomes a follower of Christ?

4. Do you promise to support the church in its worship and work, to the best of your ability?

5. Do you submit yourselves to the government and discipline of the church, and promise to study its purity and peace?

Parental Vows for Infant Baptism in the PCA

(From Book of Church Order 56-5)

1. Do you acknowledge your child's need of the cleansing blood of Jesus Christ and the renewing grace of the Holy Spirit?

2. Do you claim God's covenant promises in (his) behalf, and do you look in faith to the Lord Jesus Christ for (his) salvation as you do for your own?

3. Do you now unreservedly dedicate your child to God, and promise in humble reliance upon divine grace, that you will endeavor to set before (him) a godly example,

that you will pray with and for (him), that you will teach (him) the doctrines of our holy faith, and that you will strive by every means of God's appointment, to bring (him) up in the nurture and admonition of the Lord?

To the congregation: Do you as a congregation undertake the responsibility of assisting parents in the Christian nurture of this child?

Chapter Nine

Commonly Asked Baptism Questions

HERE I SEEK TO deal with some practical pastoral questions that are often raised. Obviously, the answers given are my own, for which I take sole responsibility.

Q 1: When is re-baptism proper? What if I was baptized in a liberal church by parents whom I know were not born again? Or what if I was baptized in a church that taught that my infant baptism conferred salvation? Should I have my baptism done again?

Answer: We believe the only time re-baptism is necessary is if you had a false baptism in the first place, that is, in a non-Trinitarian cult. All baptisms in the name of the Trinity are acknowledged by us as valid and should not be repeated. We say this even in cases of potentially corrupt theology held by the church administering it or a lack of authentic faith in parents or the minister doing the baptism. The important thing is baptism in the name of the Trinity. That fulfills the condition laid down by Christ. If we were to go back and attempt to judge the heart intentions of people from decades ago, we might have to second guess many individual baptisms.

Q 2: Pastor, I need advice. I professed faith in Christ at age 12 and joined a Presbyterian church after taking a communicants class. Since I had never previously been baptized, I received baptism then as a believer, by sprinkling. That experience was very meaningful to me. Now, a local Baptist church has offered me the position of church organist. I am well qualified for this and believe I could glorify God serving there. The leaders of that congregation are fine people, but one wrinkle in this job offer is that they tell me I must be baptized again by immersion to be hired and to join that congregation. I feel as if they're asking me to deny my previous believer's baptism, entirely over the issue of immersion. What should I do here?"

Answer: I do not see an absolute right or wrong principle ruling this decision. You are already biblically baptized, but baptistic folks are exalting a secondary matter of how much water suffices into a main principle. Your dilemma is similar to 1 Corinthians 9:19-22, about liberty of conscience in secondary matters. Paul writes: "For though I am free from all, I have made myself a servant to all, that I may win more of them" (19).

Either way you decide, you can please God in this decision. For you, it is a matter of submission to the "weaker brother." You desire to give glory to the Lord by your gifts of music, so the question is: what can your conscience be at peace with? Submitting to immersion baptism for the sake of harmony with these brethren is not wrong if you are able to approach it with a humble attitude.

If you wish to proceed with this hiring, I suggest you first write a cordial note to the pastor telling him that while you do not agree that immersion is essential, yet you are willing to submit to their rule in the matter. That would launch your staff relation on an honest footing, and hopefully they will respect you for it. If they do not accept such a statement as a prelude to you being immersed, then I'd say it is an indicator that you most likely are better off not being employed there.

Q 3: Pastor, you don't know me. I have never been in your church and I do not attend any church, but I grew up Presbyterian. Now I have a baby and my mother is pressing me hard to get her baptized. Could I arrange to bring my daughter in for you to baptize her?

Answer: This phone call comes from a young mother with no clear understanding of baptism, the gospel of salvation, or the church. She is responding to family pressure for someone to "shake a little holy water" over her baby's head, but she wants no involvement with a live congregation of Christians. It is sad when the world values religious ceremonies merely to fulfill traditions or family pressure, with no comprehension of what baptism is about.

I will gently but firmly decline the mother's request. But in doing so I will try to warmly encourage her to form a relationship with our church so that we might come to know her as a believer. If we are able to build that relationship and she discovers what it means to be Jesus' disciple, the way could later be open to baptize her child. Unfortunately, phone callers like this woman tend to quickly hang up when they hear we will not concede to their request for what I call a "drive-through sacrament."

Q 4: From a church member: Pastor, I'm calling to arrange little Robby's baptism. My husband and I wonder if you will do the ceremony at our home instead of in a Sunday church service. We're having a family reunion on April 27th, when the dogwood trees in our back yard will all be in beautiful bloom, and we'd like the ceremony to be in our garden with just family present. Is this all right?

Answer: I have to be diplomatic with this church member and decline to perform the baptism service at her home. Baptism is not a private or family-only affair. It is a sacrament of the gathered church, and it signifies in-gathering to Christ's Body on earth. If at all possible, it should be performed in the presence of worshiping people of God.

One rare occasion for which we might have a private baptism service in a hospital, nursing center, or a home, is if there is definite need to baptize someone who is physically unable to be present in a church-based service. Even then, we strive to have a few elders or other church members present to represent the wider body of Christ.

Q 5: Here is another member's inquiry I've had more than once: Pastor, I hear the emphasis being made on baptism and the Lord's Supper as New Testament replacements for Old Testament sacraments of circumcision and the Passover. But I don't understand why we do not encourage our baptized covenant children to participate in the Lord's Supper as little children did in the Passover ceremony. Isn't this inconsistent?

Answer: There are some people in Presbyterian and other Reformed congregations who believe that, as a matter of covenant consistency, even infants should receive the Lord's Supper. But the majority of us across the ages have disagreed with what we call paedocommunion. While there is no biblical mandate on the matter, we urge parents to wait until a prudent age when, as adolescents, their children can present a testimony to the Session and be admitted to the Lord's

Table. The age for this to happen is up to the discretion of every church session.

In our congregation the opportunity primarily occurs at seventh grade, when our youth pastor leads a communicants class through about ten weeks of instruction in matters related to what gospel faith in Christ is about. Then each student submits a written testimony of their personal faith. This written document becomes the basis of a brief interview of the young person with several elders that aims to be encouraging, while probing for a sense of assurance of salvation alive in each candidate

The key Scripture that guides us here is 1 Corinthians 11:28, which says, "Let a person *examine himself*, then, and so eat of the bread and drink of the cup." An infant is incapable of such self-examination. We realize some children as young as five or six might have a valid profession of faith in Jesus as Lord. However, wisdom and experience tell us to be cautious. There is no compelling reason to admit them as communicants too hastily. Communion at the Lord's Table is one of life's privileges worth waiting for, until sufficient maturity is in place for self-examination.

Q 6: Pastor, we are ready to have our new baby baptized. But as you know, years ago when our daughter who is now eight and our son who is now five were born, we did not yet believe in covenant

baptism as we do now. What do you think about our having all three children baptized together with the new baby?"

Answer: I am delighted to fulfill such a request. This is truly a "household baptism" similar to Acts 16, and I have joyfully presided over these. My own opinion has been that if the oldest child was, say, 11-12 or so – close to the age of being eligible to join a youth communicants class – I would advise for that child to be baptized as a believer, when he or she makes a personal testimony before the elders and joins the church with other youth communicants.

Q 7: Pastor, I am going to the Holy Land for a tour. I see from the tour agenda that we will be offered the opportunity to be re-baptized in the Jordan River. It seems like this could be quite thrilling, to be baptized where Jesus was. What do you think about this?"

Answer: See my response to questions 1 and 2 about re-baptism. This action is neither necessary nor helpful to your walk with Christ. Its premise is based on a mere emotional or even superstitious association with Holy Land geography. Water of the Jordan River is no more holy than any other.

ENDNOTES

[1] BENJAMIN B. WARFIELD, "The Polemics of Infant Baptism" in *Studies in Theology* (Edinburgh: Banner of Truth, 1988), 390.

[2] R. C. Sproul, *Essential Truths of the Christian Faith* (Wheaton, IL: Tyndale House, 1992), 223.

[3] Warfield, "The Doctrine of Infant Salvation" in *Studies in Theology*, 429-44.

[4] James M. Boice, *Ephesians: An Expositional Commentary* (Grand Rapids, MI: Baker Book House, 1988), 131.

[5] Francis A. Schaeffer, *Baptism* (Wilmington, DE: Cross Publishing, 1973), 8.

About the Author

 Michael Allen Rogers (D Min, Westminster Theological Seminary) served 45 years of pastoral ministry with the Presbyterian Church in America, including 25 years as senior pastor of Westminster Church, Lancaster, Pennsylvania, where he is now Pastor Emeritus.

He is also the author of *What Happens After I Die?* (Crossway, 2013).

Contact Dr. Rogers at:
michael.rogers@onekingpress.com

NOTES